Picture Dictionary

Oxford University Press
198 Madison Avenue, New York, NY 10016, USA
Great Clarendon Street, Oxford OX2 6DP, England

Oxford New York
Athens Auckland Bangkok Bogotá Buenos Aires
Cape Town Chennai Dar es Salaam Delhi Florence
Hong Kong Istanbul Karachi Kolkata Kuala Lumpur
Madrid Melbourne Mexico City Mumbai Nairobi Paris
São Paulo Singapore Taipei Tokyo Toronto Warsaw

and associated companies in
Berlin Ibadan

OXFORD is a trademark of Oxford University Press.

ISBN 0-19-435865-8

Editorial Manager: Shelagh Speers
Senior Editor: Sherri Arbogast
Editor: Lynne Robertson
Production Editor: Mark Steven Long
Elementary Design Manager: Doris Chen
Designer: Ruby Harn
Senior Art Buyer: Alexandra F. Rockafeller

Printing (last digit): 10 9 8 7 6 5

Printed in China

Acknowledgments:
To all our students who have helped us to develop
both as teachers and teacher trainers, thank you.
Without you, we could not have written this book.

To our editors at Oxford University Press, and to the
design team, thank you for your inspiration and
hard work.

An finally, to our husbands and children, thank you
for your support and understanding.

Illustrations by: Yvette Banek, Shirley Beckes/Craven
Design, Susan Detrich, Patrick Giraud, John Jones,
Anne Kennedy/HK Portfolio, Inc., Tammie Lyon,
Susan Miller, Elise Mills, Michael Morris, Pam
Peltier, Stephanie Peterson, Jenifer Schneider,
Dorothy Stott, and Jim Talbot

Cover design by: Ruby Harn

Cover illustrations by: Yvette Banek, Patrick Giraud,
Michael Morris, Pam Peltier, and Jim Talbot

Frisbee is a brand name and trademark of Wham-O,
Inc. Used with permission.

Picture Dictionary

by
R. Nakata
K. Frazier
B. Hoskins

Oxford University Press

Table of Contents

Unit 6: Play

Unit 7: Activities

Unit 8: Food

Unit 9: Community

Unit 10: Animals

Unit 11: Environment

Introduction

LET'S GO PICTURE DICTIONARY

The *Let's Go Picture Dictionary* is a full-color, topic-based dictionary for children, designed to complement the seven-level *Let's Go* course. The *Picture Dictionary* presents the words from the *Let's Go* series, plus other high-frequency vocabulary, in situations that are universal to children everywhere.

Like its parent course, the *Let's Go Picture Dictionary* features a unique question-and-answer approach that helps students develop productive language skills as they build their vocabulary. The *Picture Dictionary* can be used as a supplement to the *Let's Go* series or independently. Either way, the *Dictionary* functions as a valuable reference guide to English.

COMPONENTS

The Picture Dictionary

The *Picture Dictionary* consists of 975 high-frequency vocabulary items grouped by topic. The words and phrases are based on the vocabulary from *Let's Go* Levels 1–6 and the *Let's Go Starter* Level, plus additional topic-based vocabulary.

The Cassette

The accompanying *Cassette* contains all the vocabulary and language patterns found in the *Picture Dictionary*. All words and phrases are spoken clearly and carefully, but with natural speed and intonation, so students can become accustomed to hearing the vocabulary as it is spoken naturally.

PHILOSOPHY AND PRINCIPLES

The *Let's Go Picture Dictionary* is based on the same principles as the *Let's Go* series. From the very beginning, students are encouraged not only to learn the new vocabulary but also to interact with each other using the language pattern provided for each topic.

The full-page illustrations and language patterns in the *Picture Dictionary* feature situations from children's everyday lives. Students begin speaking English more easily when relating to these familiar experiences.

ORGANIZATION

The *Picture Dictionary* covers 55 topics in 11 units. Each topic is presented on two pages. Generally, the first page consists of a scene showing the vocabulary items in context (pictures only). The facing page features the vocabulary items in isolation (pictures with word labels). Certain topics present the vocabulary items in a slightly different format.

LANGUAGE PATTERNS

Except for Topics 1 and 2, each topic in the *Picture Dictionary* is accompanied by a language pattern that appears in an easy-to-identify shaded box. These patterns provide context for the new words, and function as models for extended language practice. You may occasionally need to modify the patterns, based on the skill level of your students.

Wherever possible, language patterns have been simplified to accommodate all the topic vocabulary. However, some language patterns may require alteration (such as changes in article usage, preposition usage, subject-verb agreement, etc.) when other vocabulary is substituted for the model vocabulary. Use these situations as learning opportunities for your students. Encourage them to discuss any required changes to the new vocabulary and/or language patterns.

LESSON PLANNING

Setting Goals

When making a lesson plan, use the language pattern and topic to help you set your goals. For example:

Topic:	Toys (Topic 28, page 52)
Language Pattern:	*Which toy do you want?* *I want a ball.*
Objectives:	to say the names of various toys to express preferences to ask others about their preferences

Making an Outline

Each lesson should contain the following five steps: Review, Present the topic, Present the vocabulary, Present the language pattern, and Extension.

1. Review

Begin each lesson by reviewing the previous lesson taught, selecting from a variety of drills, games, and activities (see the section on Other Games and Activities, page viii, for ideas). Whenever possible, use your review as a transition into the new topic. Select vocabulary items that your students already know from the current topic, and plug them into a structure taught in a previous unit. This example uses vocabulary from Topic 28, Toys:

Teacher: *Is this a ball?*
Students: *Yes, it is.*

2. Present the topic

Introduce the topic to students before they open their books. This helps the class to focus on the lesson, and it helps you to assess what vocabulary your students already know. This can be done in a variety of ways. For example:

• Draw or show pictures of items related to the topic (using picture cards from the *Let's Go* series or from other sources), or bring in real items, if possible, and ask students to identify as many of the items as they can.

• Using the items above, make statements or ask questions using structures they know. For example,
T: *I have a kite. Do you have a kite?*

• Ask students if they can list any other items they know in this category.

3. Present the vocabulary
Use the following steps to introduce the vocabulary:

a. Have students open their books.

b. Play the cassette. Have students listen and point to the pictures.

c. Play the cassette again. Have students repeat the words aloud. Play the cassette section again, as necessary. Or, model the words for the students yourself. Give students ample opportunity to hear each word and practice its pronunciation.

You can also reinforce the new vocabulary by means of an appropriate drill or activity. For example:

• Use Total Physical Response (TPR). Give a command using the new vocabulary item. Students act out the command, but are not expected to repeat the item at this stage. This is especially useful in teaching verbs.

• Describe a word and have students identify it by pointing to it on the page. For example, T: *It looks like a diamond. It can fly. It's a kite.* Students locate the kite in the full-page illustration and point to it.

• Ask simple Yes/No or "or" questions to allow students to give one-word responses. T: *Who has the yo-yo? Sam or Ginger?*

4. Present the language pattern
The students can use the language pattern to practice talking about the vocabulary items presented in the illustrations. There are two types of language patterns in the *Picture Dictionary*. Use the following steps to present them:

Type 1: Question-and answer-patterns
This is the most common pattern used in the *Picture Dictionary*. For example:

S1: *Which toy do you want?*
S2: *I want a ball.*

a. Model the language pattern for the students. (Note: You should focus first on the answer before presenting the question and the answer in combination.) Say the answer. Have the class repeat after you. Model and repeat several times.

b. When students have thoroughly practiced the answer, model the question and answer together, either by using the cassette or by saying the pattern yourself. Have the class repeat the question and answer several times.

c. Divide the class into two groups. Have Group A ask the question, and Group B answer. Then have groups switch roles. (Practicing in two groups, within the secure setting of speaking with other students, allows the students to become more familiar with the patterns.)

d. Put the students into pairs or small groups, and have them practice asking each other questions about the picture. (Practicing in pairs or small groups is an ideal way for students to learn from one another, since they can share information.)

Type 2: Command patterns
Command patterns are found in Topic 10, Parts of the Body, and Topic 26, Classroom Verbs. For example,
T: *Point to your head.*

a. Model the language pattern for the students, either by using the cassette or by saying it yourself. Perform the physical action as you say the phrase. Have the class repeat as they perform the action. Demonstrate and repeat several times.

b. Put the students into pairs or small groups, and have them practice giving the commands and performing the actions.

5. Extension
Have students close their books. Extend and reinforce the topic and the new vocabulary with activities and games. See below for activity and game ideas.

ACTIVITIES USING THE ILLUSTRATIONS

You can use the many illustrations in the *Picture Dictionary* with a wide range of language tasks to help students practice the language they have learned.

Talking
Have students talk about the full-page illustrations by using the language structures they have already learned. Students can either make statements about the page or express their own opinions, depending on their ability. Some examples using vocabulary from Topic 31, Sports, follow:

• You can have lower-level students point to the objects they know in the illustration and say the words or simple sentences:

S1: *I like tennis.*
S2: *This is a soccer ball.*

• You can elicit more difficult sentences from higher-level students:

S1: *They are playing golf.*
S2: *I like to play basketball.*

See "Dialogues" and "Storytelling," below, for further Talking activities.

Writing
The full-page illustrations can be used as springboards for various kinds of writing activities. Some examples follow:

• This activity exposes students to proper sentence formation and mechanics in a very controlled, simplified manner. Have each student make one sentence about the illustration. Write it down on a piece of paper and return it to the student. The student then copies the sentence and draws a picture to illustrate it. Finally, the student reads the sentence aloud to the class and displays his or her picture.

• With higher-level students, you can have each student write several sentences about the picture and, if desired, illustrate them. Students then read their sentences aloud to the class.

• This activity teaches students awareness of the logical order of sentences. While it may be challenging, students will always find it interesting since they are generating their own prose. Have each student write one simple sentence based on the full-page scene. Then create group prose by having students put their sentences together. This example uses vocabulary from Topic 51, The Zoo:

S1: *I saw lions and pandas.*
S2: *There was a whale in the water.*
S3: *I went to the zoo.*
S4: *I like the zoo.*

Write the sentences on the board. Then, have the class alter and rearrange the sentences to make them more sequential. (Prompt when necessary.) For example:

I went to the zoo. I saw lions and pandas. There was a whale in the water. I like the zoo!

Students then copy the new paragraph and illustrate it, if desired.

Dialogues

Higher-level students can work in pairs or small groups to develop dialogues for each scene. They name the characters and then create a dialogue. This example uses vocabulary from Topic 30, Birthday Party:
Julie (birthday girl): *There are seven candles.*
Tom (boy on left): *Happy birthday!*
Tina (girl on right): *Let's sing!*
All children: (singing) *Happy birthday to you, …*

Have the pairs or small groups perform their dialogues for the class.

Storytelling

Higher-level students can work in pairs or small groups to make stories for the scenes. Hold up the *Dictionary* and ask the class questions; for example, T: (point to page 40) *They are packing their clothes. Where are they going? What will they do? What will they need?*
Put students into pairs or groups. Have them write stories about the picture based on your questions. Then, have them read their stories to the class. This example uses vocabulary from Topic 22, Clothes:

This is John. He is going on a homestay. He hasn't finished packing yet. He is going to Hawaii. It will be hot. He will need some T-shirts.

Let the students refer to their books or use other resources to get ideas for sentences. Be sure to circulate and help groups with any words they don't know.

OTHER GAMES AND ACTIVITIES

Find the Picture
This activity works with topics that feature a full-page illustration. Separate students into pairs. S1 points to one of the numbered illustrations on the right-hand page (where vocabulary is depicted in isolation). S2 must find the matching item in the full-page illustration, and say the word or phrase. Then students switch roles.

Find Sam and Ginger
Sam and Ginger, the *Let's Go* cats, appear in the full-page illustration in the first topic in every unit (Topics 1, 10, 15, 22, 25, 28, 31, 36, 42, 48, 52, 54, and 55). Have students try to find them and create sentences about them. Ask questions to prompt students, if necessary. For example, T: *Where is Ginger? What is she doing? Where is Sam? What is he wearing?*, etc.

Who's the Fastest?
This activity uses the numbered lists of vocabulary items. Have two students compete to say all the words as fast as possible. One student starts at item number 1 and works down. The other student starts at the last numbered item and works up. When you signal for the race to begin, both students work through the list at the same time, reading each word as fast as possible. The first student to reach the other's start word first wins.

For greater challenge, when students meet at the same word, they have to play Even Odd (the Paper-Rock-Scissors game). The winner gets to advance. The loser must start over from his or her beginning word again.

Find the Word
Students can do this activity either in teams or in pairs, using the numbered list of words. Call out a word (or have a volunteer do so). The first student to locate the word on the page gets a point.

Find the Card
Use picture cards from either the *Let's Go* series or another source. Have at least one card for each student. Spread the cards on the floor facedown. Divide the class into two teams, and have teams stand on either side of the cards. Say one of the vocabulary items from the *Picture Dictionary*. Each student picks up one card. The student who picks up the card with the matching vocabulary item keeps it. Then, the other students put down their cards, mix them quickly, and play the game again. When the game is over, the team with the most cards wins. For reading practice, this activity can be done using teacher-made word cards.

Find Your Partner

This activity requires pairs of *Let's Go* picture cards (or picture cards from another source) and teacher-made word cards. Give each student either a picture card or a word card. Students move around the room; each student must find the student holding the corresponding word or picture card. Lower-level students can simply show their cards to each other. Higher-level students can keep their cards hidden and ask questions to find their partners. For example:

S1: *Do you like tennis?* or *Do you have a cat?*
S2: *Yes, I do./No, I don't.*

Spell It

This activity can be done in small groups or with the whole class. Spell out a word (or have a volunteer do so). Students compete to find it in the numbered word list, or in the full-page illustration, and then say the word.

Alphabetizing Activity

Students work in pairs or small groups to sort the topic words in alphabetical order. They can write the words down on a separate sheet of paper or take turns writing them on the board.

Word Discovery Activity

Working in small groups or pairs, students find words in a topic that fit the parameters you describe. For example, ask students to:

*   find all the words that start with a certain sound, such as *r, th,* or an initial vowel sound;

*   find all the words that end in *-d* or *-th,* or words that contain a short vowel sound (medial position);

*   identify nouns that take *an;*

*   identify parts of speech, such as nouns, verbs, or prepositions.

You can have students write the words down or say them aloud. Or, you can have teams race to write as many of the words as they can, either on the board or on a team list.

Sentence Writing

Using the numbered word lists, students make sentences for each word (other than the sentence in the language pattern). They can do this orally, in writing, in pairs, or alone. Have students share their sentences with the class. For added challenge, have students make riddles; for example, S1: *This animal is tall. It has a very long neck. It has spots. What is it?*

Make Crossword Puzzles

Have students work in pairs to create their own crossword puzzles, using words from the numbered word lists. Each pair can then exchange their puzzle with another pair.

Find New Words

Divide the class into teams. Teams look at the full-page illustration and identify as many objects as they can that are not listed in the numbered word list. The team listing the most words wins.

Categories

This is a good review activity. Divide the class into small groups. Gather word cards or picture cards from several topics. Review the vocabulary by mixing the cards and having students group them into categories. This activity can be as simple or complex as you wish. For example:

*   Combine word or picture cards for vocabulary from two topics; for example, Topic 37, Vegetables and Topic 50, Forest Animals. Have students separate the cards into the two categories, in this case, animals and food.

*   Combine word cards from one or more topics. Have students categorize the cards based on initial letter, number of syllables, alphabetical order, etc.

*   Combine picture cards from one or more topic. Have students categorize the cards based on item color or size.

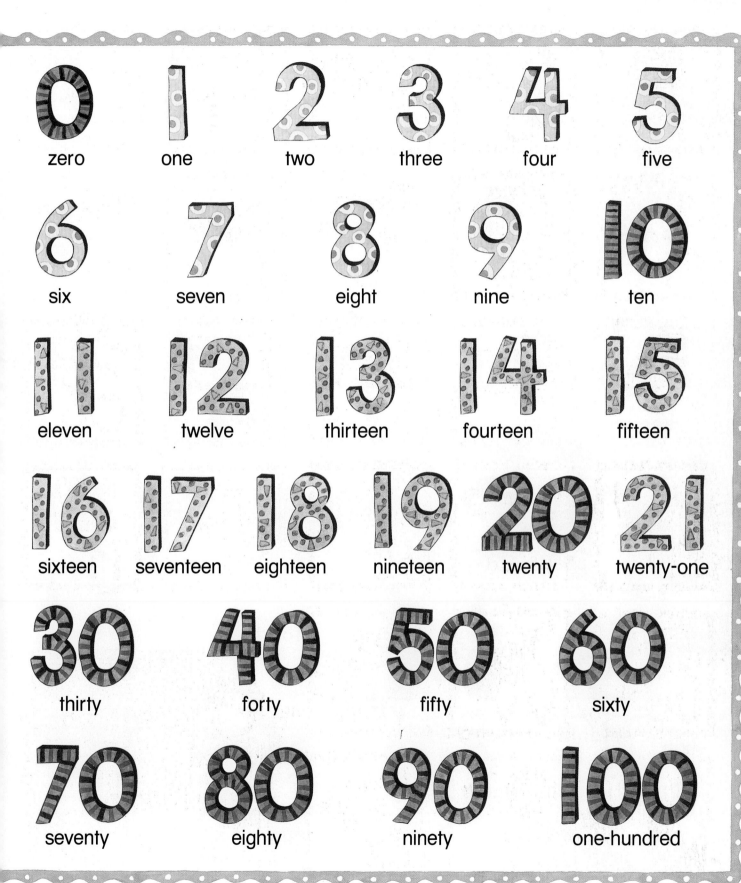

0 zero
1 one
2 two
3 three
4 four
5 five

6 six
7 seven
8 eight
9 nine
10 ten

11 eleven
12 twelve
13 thirteen
14 fourteen
15 fifteen

16 sixteen
17 seventeen
18 eighteen
19 nineteen
20 twenty
21 twenty-one

30 thirty
40 forty
50 fifty
60 sixty

70 seventy
80 eighty
90 ninety
100 one-hundred

Who's first?
She is.

first

second

third

fourth

fifth

sixth

seventh

eighth

ninth

tenth

What's the date today?
It's Monday, January 4th.

The Months

January	July
February	August
March	September
April	October
May	November
June	December

Days of the Week

Sunday	Thursday
Monday	Friday
Tuesday	Saturday
Wednesday	

The Seasons

spring

summer

fall

winter

What time is it?
It's one o'clock.

1. one o'clock

2. one fifteen

3. one thirty

4. one forty-five

5. two o'clock

6. twelve ten

7. five fifty-five

8. morning

9. afternoon

10. evening

11. noon

12. midnight

13. day

14. night

What shape is this?
It's a circle.

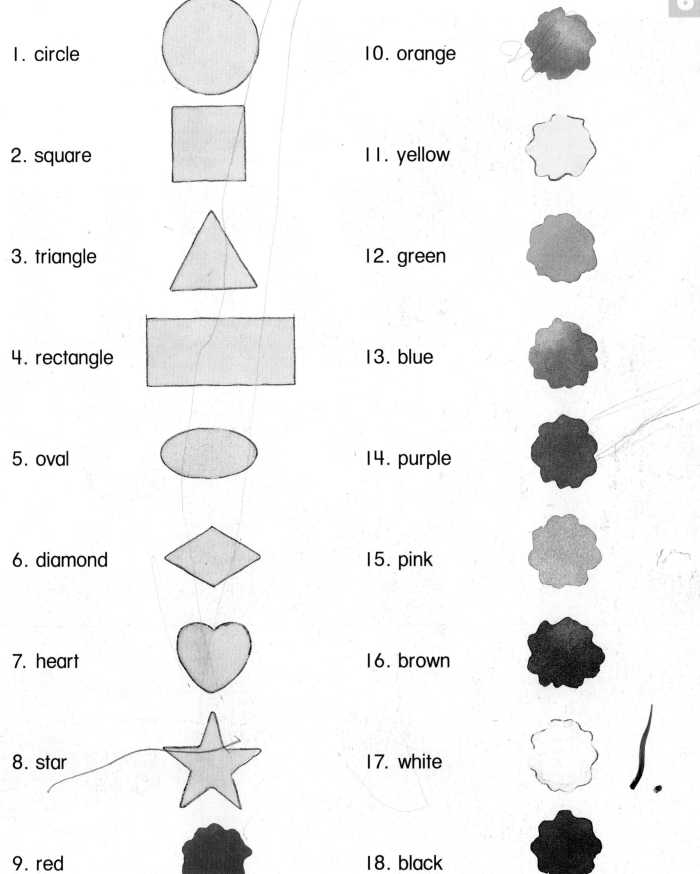

1. circle

2. square

3. triangle

4. rectangle

5. oval

6. diamond

7. heart

8. star

9. red

10. orange

11. yellow

12. green

13. blue

14. purple

15. pink

16. brown

17. white

18. black

Is it empty?
No, it's full.

1. empty

2. full

3. round

4. square

5. cold

6. hot

7. new

8. old

9. short

10. long

11. light

12. heavy

13. big

14. little

15. soft

16. hard

17. dirty

18. clean

19. wet

20. dry

What's the opposite of neat?
Messy.

12

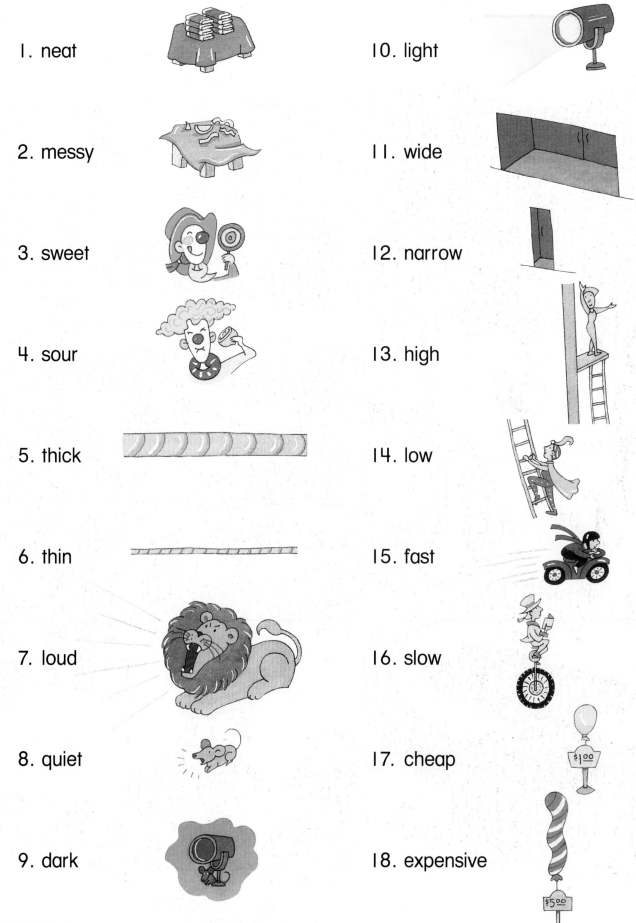

1. neat

2. messy

3. sweet

4. sour

5. thick

6. thin

7. loud

8. quiet

9. dark

10. light

11. wide

12. narrow

13. high

14. low

15. fast

16. slow

17. cheap

18. expensive

Where is he?
He's in the tunnel.

1. in

8. across from

2. out of

9. between

3. to the left of

10. next to

4. to the right of

11. under

5. in front of

12. on

6. behind

13. going up

7. by

14. going down

Point to your head.

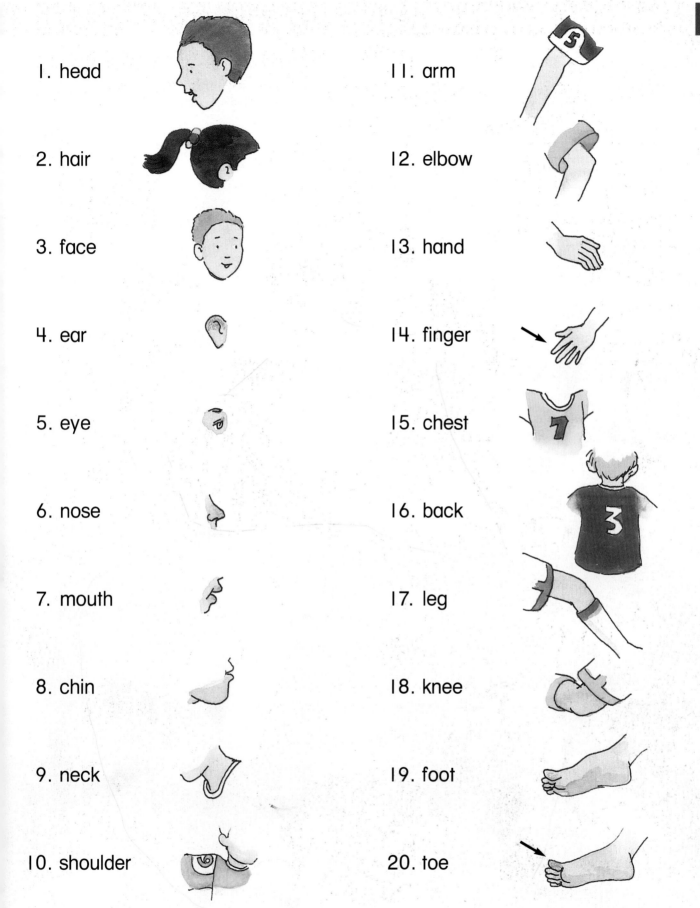

1. head

2. hair

3. face

4. ear

5. eye

6. nose

7. mouth

8. chin

9. neck

10. shoulder

11. arm

12. elbow

13. hand

14. finger

15. chest

16. back

17. leg

18. knee

19. foot

20. toe

What does he look like?
He has red hair. He's cute.

1. red hair

2. brown hair

3. black hair

4. blond hair

5. gray hair

6. curly hair

7. straight hair

8. brown eyes

9. black eyes

10. blue eyes

11. green eyes

12. pretty

13. cute

14. ugly

15. fat

16. thin

17. young

18. old

19. tall

20. short

What are you doing?
I'm washing my face.

1. wash my face

2. take a bath

3. brush my teeth

4. comb my hair

5. sneeze

6. blow my nose

7. cry

8. chew

9. yawn

10. sleep

11. scratch my back

12. stretch my arms

13. clap my hands

14. snap my fingers

15. bend my knees

16. stamp my feet

17. wiggle my toes

18. wink

19. smile

20. laugh

What's the matter?
I have an insect bite.

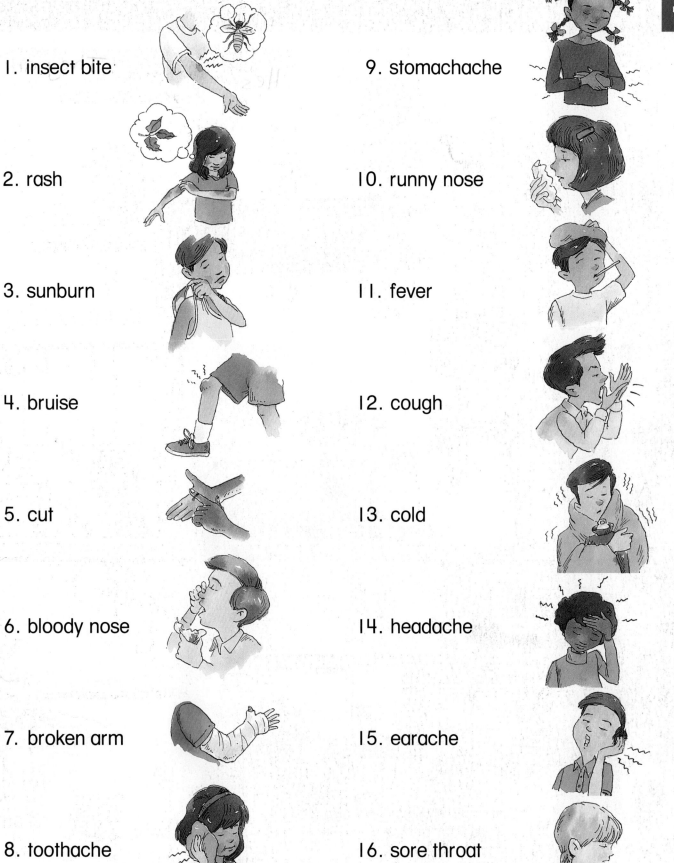

1. insect bite

2. rash

3. sunburn

4. bruise

5. cut

6. bloody nose

7. broken arm

8. toothache

9. stomachache

10. runny nose

11. fever

12. cough

13. cold

14. headache

15. earache

16. sore throat

How does he feel?
He's excited.

SNACKS

WELCOME!

COME AGAIN!

1. excited

2. happy

3. sleepy

4. sad

5. bored

6. hot

7. cold

8. hungry

9. thirsty

10. angry

11. dizzy

12. sick

13. worried

14. scared

15. embarrassed

16. surprised

He's
my

Who's she?
She's my mother.

They are

1. mother

2. father

3. sister

4. brother

5. grandmother

6. grandfather

7. aunt

8. uncle

9. cousin

10. parents

11. grandparents

12. me

Does the house have a chimney?
Yes, it does.

1. chimney

2. roof

3. steps

4. porch

5. mailbox

6. front yard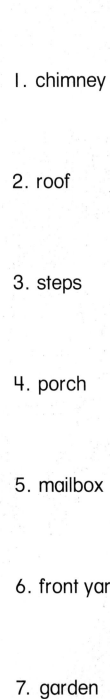

7. garden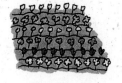

8. flowers

9. tree

10. garage

11. driveway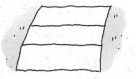

12. parking space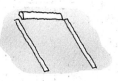

13. sidewalk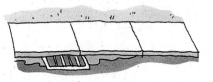

14. stairs

15. balcony

16. window

17. door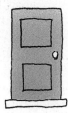

18. doorbell

What's in the kitchen?
There's a sink.

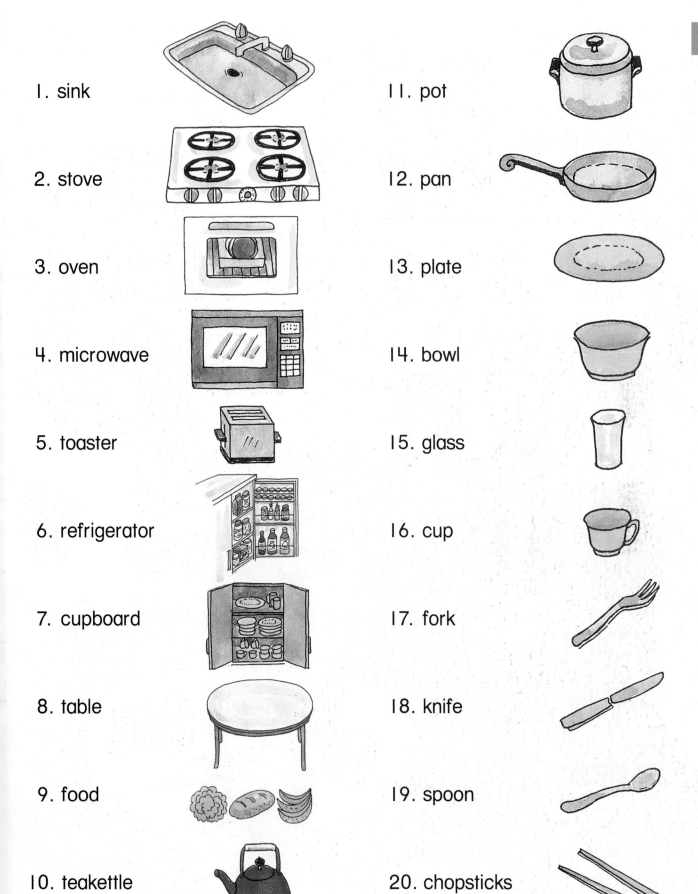

1. sink

2. stove

3. oven

4. microwave

5. toaster

6. refrigerator

7. cupboard

8. table

9. food

10. teakettle

11. pot

12. pan

13. plate

14. bowl

15. glass

16. cup

17. fork

18. knife

19. spoon

20. chopsticks

Where's the armchair?
It's near the fireplace.

1. armchair

2. sofa

3. coffee table

4. TV

5. VCR

6. videotape

7. stereo

8. cassette player

9. CD player

10. radio

11. telephone

12. bookcase

13. fireplace

14. picture

15. plant

16. air conditioner

17. carpet

18. floor

19. wall

20. ceiling

What do they have in their bedroom?
They have a toy box.

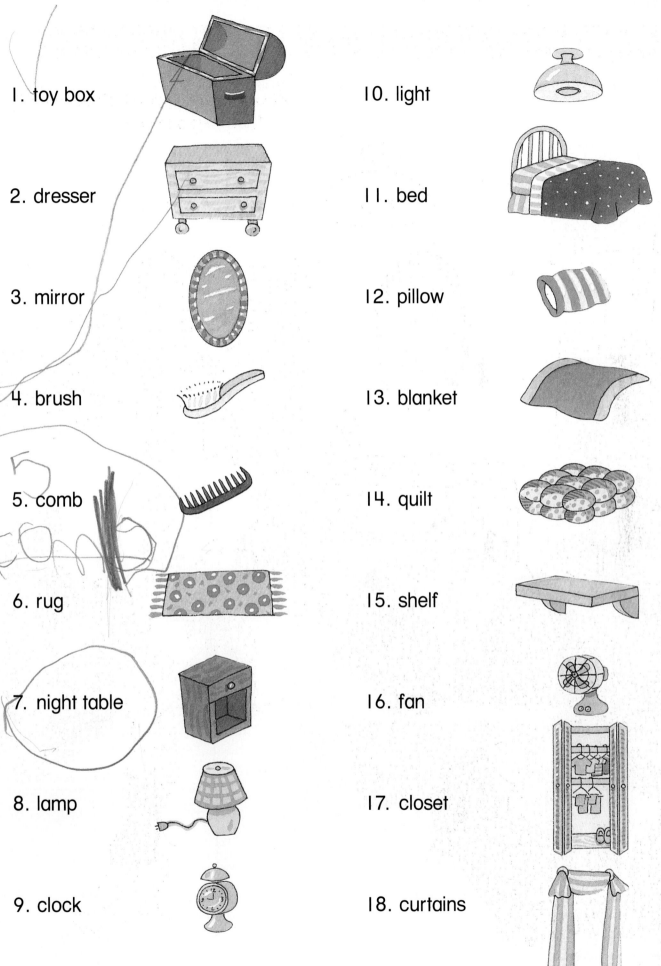

1. toy box

2. dresser

3. mirror

4. brush

5. comb

6. rug

7. night table

8. lamp

9. clock

10. light

11. bed

12. pillow

13. blanket

14. quilt

15. shelf

16. fan

17. closet

18. curtains

Can you see a toothbrush in the bathroom?
Yes, I can.

1. toothbrush

2. toothpaste

3. shampoo

4. soap

5. washcloth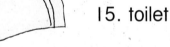

6. towel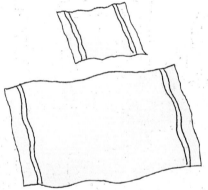

7. lotion

8. tissue

9. bandage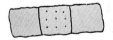

10. bathtub

11. bubble bath

12. bath mat

13. shower

14. faucet

15. toilet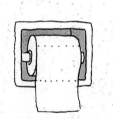

16. toilet paper

17. scale

18. wastebasket

What does she have to do?
She has to clean up.

1. clean up

2. sweep the floor

3. mop the floor

4. vacuum the carpet

5. dust the furniture

6. change the sheets

7. do the laundry

8. fold the laundry

9. put the groceries away

10. take out the trash

11. set the table

12. clear the table

13. wash the dishes

14. dry the dishes

15. feed the dog

16. walk the dog

17. turn on the light

18. turn off the light

What are you wearing?
I'm wearing a T-shirt.

1. T-shirt

2. shirt

3. pants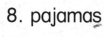

4. suit

5. vest

6. undershirt

7. underpants

8. pajamas

9. socks

10. shoes

11. sweatshirt

12. sweatpants

13. blouse

14. skirt

15. dress

16. sweater

17. tights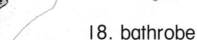

18. bathrobe

19. nightgown

20. slippers

What did you find?
I found a jacket!

1. jacket

2. coat

3. raincoat

4. jeans

5. overalls

6. sneakers

7. boots

8. hiking boots

9. sandals

10. shorts

11. swimsuit

12. uniform

13. cap

14. hat

15. glasses

16. zipper

17. pocket

18. button

What do you want to buy?
I want to buy a belt.

1. belt

2. scarf

3. necktie

4. purse

5. bag

6. umbrella

7. gloves

8. mittens

9. sunglasses

10. earrings

11. necklace

12. bracelet

13. ring

14. watch

15. key chain

16. wallet

17. barrette

18. headband

19. bow

20. handkerchief

Where's the gym?
It's next to the lunchroom.

1. gym

2. hall

3. girls' room

4. boys' room

5. lunchroom

6. music room

7. library

8. office

9. classroom

10. flag

11. desk

12. chair

13. board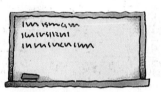

14. bulletin board

15. globe

16. computer

1. Come here.

2. Go to the door.

Please come here.

3. Look at the board.

4. Touch the desk.

5. Raise your hand.

6. Put your hand down.

7. Open your book.

8. Close your book.

9. Write your name.

10. Draw a picture.

11. Point to the window.

12. Pick up your pencil.

13. Take out your book.

14. Put your book away.

15. Stand up.

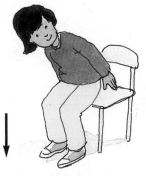

16. Sit down.

17. Be quiet.

18. Listen carefully.

19. Make two lines.

20. Count the boys.

Where's the glue?
Here it is.

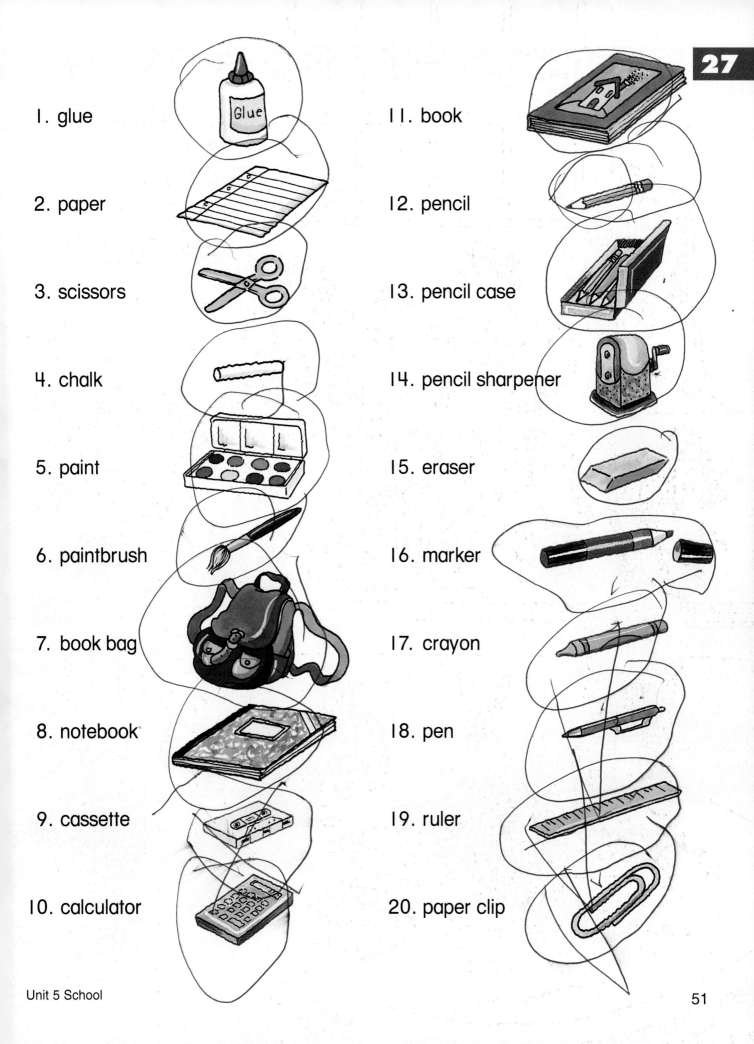

1. glue

2. paper

3. scissors

4. chalk

5. paint

6. paintbrush

7. book bag

8. notebook

9. cassette

10. calculator

11. book

12. pencil

13. pencil case

14. pencil sharpener

15. eraser

16. marker

17. crayon

18. pen

19. ruler

20. paper clip

Which toy do you want?
I want a ball.

1. ball

2. yo-yo

3. train

4. car

5. bicycle

6. truck

7. puzzle

8. blocks

9. robot

10. doll

11. teddy bear

12. computer game

13. hula hoop

14. kite

15. jump rope

16. skateboard

17. in-line skates

18. roller skates

What's she doing?
She's playing hopscotch.

1. play hopscotch

2. do a cartwheel

3. do a somersault

4. play with a yo-yo

5. jump rope

6. bounce a ball

7. hop on one foot

8. sit on the seesaw

9. swing on the swing

10. throw a ball

11. hit a ball

12. catch a ball

13. kick a ball

14. climb a jungle gym

15. slide down the slide

16. run a race

17. throw a Frisbee disc

18. climb a tree

19. skip

20. walk

What do you see?
    I see a birthday cake.

1. birthday cake

2. candle

3. ice cream

4. birthday card

5. present

6. wrapping paper

7. ribbon

8. balloon

9. streamer

10. tablecloth

11. party hat

12. goodie bag

13. noisemaker

14. stickers

15. beanbag

16. camera

What's your favorite sport?
Baseball.

1. baseball

2. softball

3. football

4. soccer

5. basketball

6. volleyball

7. ice hockey

8. swimming

9. badminton

10. tennis

11. bowling

12. golf

13. archery

14. track and field

15. boxing

16. wrestling

17. karate

18. gymnastics

What do you need?
I need a tennis racket.

1. tennis racket

2. tennis ball

3. baseball bat

4. baseball

5. glove

6. golf club

7. golf ball

8. basketball

9. volleyball

10. soccer ball

11. tent

12. sleeping bag

13. ice skates

14. skis

15. ski poles

16. canoe

17. paddle

18. life jacket

What do you like doing?
I like jogging.

1. jogging

2. roller-skating

3. riding a bike

4. flying a kite

5. hiking

6. camping

7. having a campfire

8. horseback riding

9. bird-watching

10. looking at the stars

11. fishing

12. canoeing

13. kayaking

14. sailing

15. surfing

16. scuba diving

17. waterskiing

18. windsurfing

19. ice-skating

20. skiing

What did she do last weekend?
She played table tennis.

1. play table tennis

2. dance

3. watch TV

4. play video games

5. use the computer

6. practice the piano

7. talk on the telephone

8. play cards

9. read a book

10. study

11. write a letter

12. collect stamps

13. do a puzzle

14. play a game

15. make a model

16. do a magic trick

17. color

18. sew

19. listen to music

20. take a nap

What does he play?
He plays the piano.

1. piano

2. guitar

3. violin

4. cello

5. recorder

6. flute

7. clarinet

8. saxophone

9. trumpet

10. trombone

11. French horn

12. tuba

13. harp

14. xylophone

15. drum

16. cymbals

What fruit do you like?
I like strawberries.

1. strawberries

2. blueberries

3. cherries

4. grapes

5. apple

6. pear

7. peach

8. plum

9. watermelon

10. melon

11. orange

12. grapefruit

13. lemon

14. lime

15. banana

16. coconut

17. pineapple

18. kiwi

19. papaya

20. mango

What do you want?
I want some peas.

1. peas

2. beans

3. lettuce

4. spinach

5. cabbage

6. cauliflower

7. broccoli

8. celery

9. asparagus

10. carrot

11. tomato

12. eggplant

13. cucumber

14. potato

15. corn

16. mushroom

17. radish

18. pepper

19. garlic

20. onion

What do you want for dinner?
I want chicken.

1. chicken

2. turkey

3. duck

4. steak

5. pork

6. ham

7. bacon

8. squid

9. oyster

10. fish

11. clam

12. shrimp

13. lobster

14. crab

Do you like pizza?
Yes, I do.

1. pizza

2. spaghetti

3. hamburger

4. french fries

5. hot dog

6. salad

7. taco

8. burrito

9. sandwich

10. sushi

11. noodles

12. rice

13. tofu

14. pancakes

15. egg

16. bread

17. butter

18. cheese

POW

19. cereal

20. yogurt

What do you like?
I like potato chips.

SODA

POTATO CHIPS

POPCORN CORN

1. potato chips

2. popcorn

3. cotton candy

4. candy

5. cookies

6. pie

7. cake

8. pudding

9. ice cream cone

10. milk

11. chocolate milk

12. lemonade

13. orange juice

14. soda pop

15. water

16. hot chocolate

17. coffee

18. tea

What's she doing?
She's washing the spinach.

1. wash the spinach

2. cut the carrots

3. slice the cucumber

4. mix the dressing

5. peel the potatoes

6. chop the onion

7. steam the vegetables

8. stir the soup

9. grill the chicken

10. bake the cookies

11. pour the oil

12. fry the fish

13. boil the water

14. drink juice

15. eat a snack

16. crack the egg

17. toast the bread

18. make breakfast

19. pack a lunch

20. cook dinner

How are they going?
They're going by car.

1. car

2. van

3. truck

4. motorcycle

5. scooter

6. taxi

7. bus

8. subway

9. train

10. fire engine

11. ambulance

12. police car

13. airplane

14. helicopter

15. sailboat

16. ship

Where's he going?
He's going to the library.

1. library

2. school

3. museum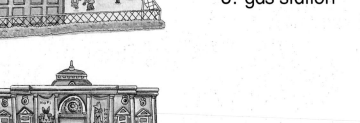

4. post office

5. hospital

6. bank

7. office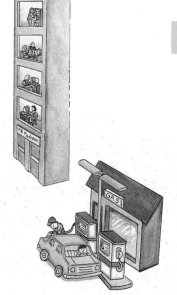

8. gas station

9. police station

10. fire station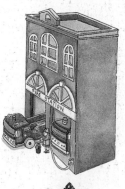

11. train station

12. factory

Where's the bookstore?
It's next to the toy store.

Supermarket

Video Store

Convenience Store

Bakery

SALE

½ PRICE Lettuce

Department Store

OPEN

Book Store

Hair Salon

Elephants In Hollywood

Movie Theater

Tickets

Flower Shop

Toy Store

OPEN

OPEN

TAXI

TAXI

Restaurant

1. bookstore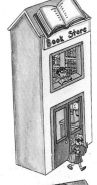

2. video store

3. flower shop

4. hair salon

5. supermarket

6. movie theater

7. bakery

8. restaurant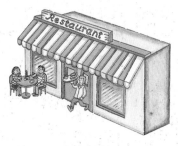

9. convenience store

10. toy store

11. department store

12. airport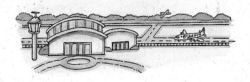

Is she a cook?
Yes, she is.

man - he
woman - she

1. cook

2. baker

3. salesclerk

4. shopkeeper

5. florist

6. bank teller

7. businessperson

8. secretary

9. factory worker

10. nurse

11. doctor

12. dentist

13. mail carrier

14. firefighter

15. police officer

16. taxi driver

17. veterinarian

18. pharmacist

19. fisherman

20. farmer

What do you want to be?
I want to be an astronaut.

1. astronaut

2. pilot

3. weather forecaster

4. news reporter

5. artist

6. photographer

7. singer

8. movie star

9. coach

10. programmer

11. engineer

12. scientist

13. student

14. teacher

15. principal

16. librarian

17. construction worker

18. carpenter

19. mechanic

20. garbage collector

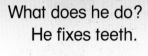
What does he do?
He fixes teeth.

1. fix teeth

2. help sick people

3. teach math

4. take pictures

5. act in movies

6. sing songs

7. paint pictures

8. sell flowers

9. grow vegetables

10. catch fish

11. collect garbage

12. make things

13. do experiments

14. build houses

15. design bridges

16. repair cars

17. drive a taxi

18. fly airplanes

19. fight fires

20. report the news

SHOW and TELL

Do you have a pet?
Yes, I have a parrot.

1. parrot

2. canary

3. cat

4. kitten

5. dog

6. puppy

7. bunny

8. gerbil

9. guinea pig

10. hamster

11. ferret

12. goldfish

13. lizard

14. turtle

Have you ever fed a pig?
Yes, I have.

1. pig

2. piglet

3. rooster

4. hen

5. chick

6. sheep

7. lamb

8. goose

9. gosling

10. cow

11. calf

12. goat

13. kid

14. duck

15. duckling

16. horse

17. foal

18. donkey

Have you ever seen a bat?
Yes, I have.

1. bat

2. owl

3. spider

4. snake

5. frog

6. mole

7. mouse

8. chipmunk

9. rabbit

10. fox

11. raccoon

12. skunk

13. squirrel

14. porcupine

15. eagle

16. moose

17. deer

18. bear

Unit 10 Animals

Where's the whale?
It's in the water.

1. whale

2. dolphin

3. seal

4. penguin

5. polar bear

6. kangaroo

7. koala

8. panda

9. camel

10. alligator

11. monkey

12. gorilla

13. tiger

14. lion

15. cheetah

16. hippopotamus

17. rhinoceros

18. zebra

19. giraffe

20. elephant

How's the weather?
It's sunny.

1. sunny

2. rainy

3. cloudy

4. windy

5. snowy

6. foggy

7. stormy

8. humid

9. hot

10. cold

11. warm

12. cool

13. lightning

14. thunder

Where do you want to go?
I want to go to the mountains.

1. mountains

2. volcano

3. waterfall

4. hill

5. forest

6. field

7. desert

8. lake

9. island

10. river

11. beach

12. sea

13. harbor

14. village

15. farm

16. city

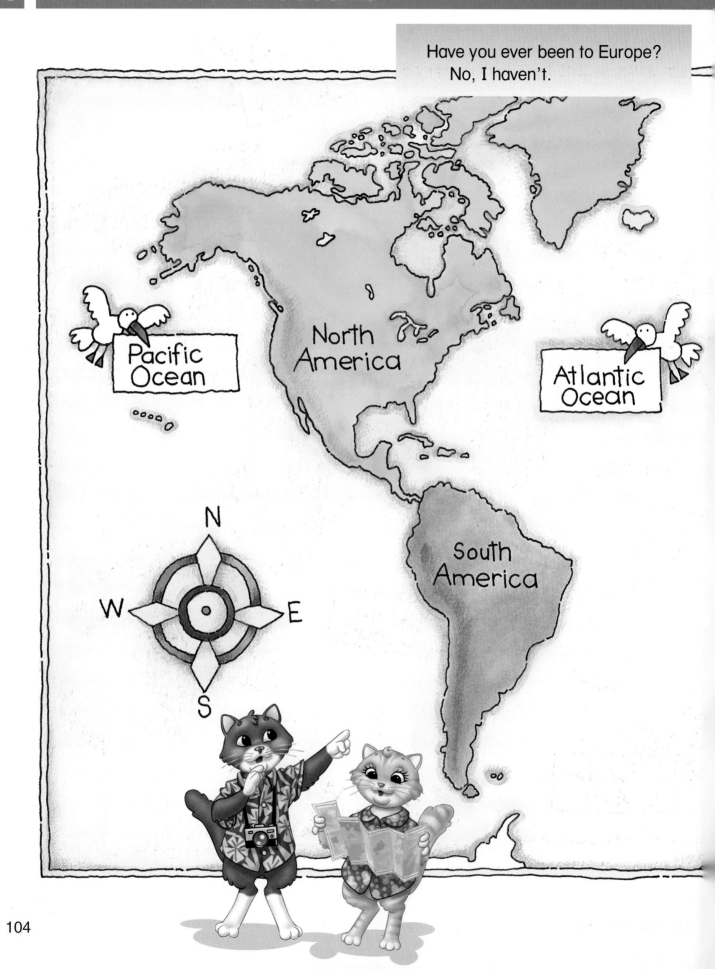

Have you ever been to Europe?
No, I haven't.

Pacific Ocean

North America

Atlantic Ocean

South America

N
W   E
S

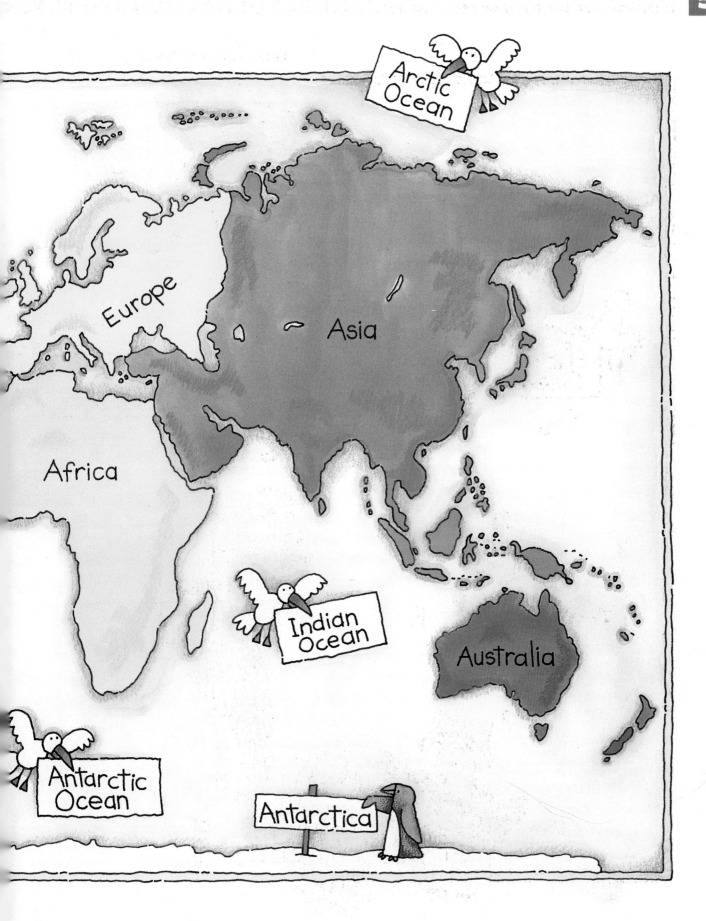

Arctic Ocean

Europe

Asia

Africa

Indian Ocean

Australia

Antarctic Ocean

Antarctica

What's that?
It's Earth.

star

Mars

Venus

Mercury

Sun

telescope

rocket

Pluto

Neptune

Saturn

Uranus

Moon

Earth

Jupiter

Word List

This is a complete alphabetical listing of the words and phrases that appear in the *Let's Go Picture Dictionary*. Some of the vocabulary items in this list are followed by two numbers. The boldfaced number refers to the page where the word or phrase appears. The second number refers to its location on the vocabulary page. For example, "balloon **57** / 8" means that the word *balloon* is item number 8 on page 57. Vocabulary items featured in more than one topic have a separate listing for each topic.

A a

accessories **42**
across from **15** / 8
act in movies **90** / 5
activities **62**
Africa **105**
afternoon **7** / 9
air conditioner **33** / 16
airplane **81** / 13
airport **85** / 12
alligator **99** / 10
alphabet **2**
ambulance **81** / 11
and **8**
angry **25** / 10
animals **94**
Antarctica **105**
apartment **28**
apple **69** / 5
April **5**
archery **59** / 13
Arctic Ocean **104**
arm **17** / 11
armchair **33** / 1
artist **88** / 5
Asia **105**
asparagus **71** / 9
astronaut **88** / 1
Atlantic Ocean **104**

August **5**
aunt **27** / 7
Australia **105**

B b

back **17** / 16
bacon **73** / 7
badminton **58** / 9
bag **45** / 5
bake the cookies **79** / 10
baker **86** / 2
bakery **85** / 7
balcony **29** / 15
ball **53** / 1
balloon **57** / 8
banana **69** / 15
bandage **37** / 9
bank **83** / 6
bank teller **86** / 6
barrette **45** / 17
baseball (Sports) **58** / 1
baseball (Sports
　　Equipment) **61** / 4
baseball bat **61** / 3
basketball (Sports) **58** / 5
basketball (Sports
　　Equipment) **61** / 8
bat **97** / 1
bath mat **37** / 12

bathrobe **41** / 18
bathroom **36**
bathtub **37** / 10
be quiet **49** / 17
beach **103** / 11
beanbag **57** / 15
beans **71** / 2
bear **97** / 18
bed **35** / 11
bedroom **34**
behind **15** / 6
belt **45** / 1
bend my knees **21** / 15
between **15** / 9
bicycle **53** / 5
big **11** / 13
bird-watching **62** / 9
birthday cake **57** / 1
birthday card **57** / 4
birthday party **56**
black **9** / 18
black eyes **19** / 9
black hair **19** / 3
blanket **35** / 13
blocks **53** / 8
blond hair **19** / 4
bloody nose **23** / 6
blouse **41** / 13
blow my nose **20** / 6
blue **9** / 13

blue eyes 19 / 10

blueberries 69 / 2

board 47 / 13

body 16

boil the water 79 / 13

book 51 / 11

book bag 51 / 7

bookcase 33 / 12

bookstore 85 / 1

boots 43 / 7

bored 25 / 5

bounce a ball 54 / 6

bow 45 / 19

bowl 31 / 14

bowling 59 / 11

boxing 59 / 15

boy's room 47 / 4

bracelet 45 / 12

bread 75 / 16

broccoli 71 / 7

broken arm 23 / 7

brother 27 / 4

brown 9 / 16

brown eyes 19 / 8

brown hair 19 / 2

bruise 23 / 4

brush 35 / 4

brush my teeth 20 / 1

bubble bath 37 / 11

build houses 91 / 14

buildings 82

bulletin board 47 / 14

bunny 93 / 7

burrito 74 / 8

bus 81 / 7

businessperson 86 / 7

butter 75 / 17

button 43 / 18

by 15 / 7

C c

cabbage 71 / 5

cake 77 / 7

calculator 51 / 10

calendar 5

calf 95 / 11

camel 99 / 9

camera 57 / 16

camping 62 / 6

canary 93 / 2

candle 57 / 2

candy 77 / 4

canoe 61 / 16

canoeing 63 / 12

cap 43 / 13

car (Toys) 53 / 4

car (Transportation) 81 / 1

carpenter 89 / 18

carpet 33 / 17

carrot 71 / 10

cassette 51 / 9

cassette player 33 / 8

cat 93 / 3

catch a ball 55 / 12

catch fish 91 / 10

cauliflower 71 / 6

CD player 33 / 9

ceiling 33 / 20

celery 71 / 8

cello 67 / 4

cereal 75 / 19

chair 47 / 12

chalk 51 / 4

change the sheets 38 / 6

cheap 13 / 17

cheese 75 / 18

cheetah 99 / 15

cherries 69 / 3

chest 17 / 15

chew 20 / 8

chick 95 / 5

chicken 73 / 1

chimney 29 / 1

chin 17 / 8

chipmunk 97 / 8

chocolate milk 77 / 11

chop the onion 78 / 6

chopsticks 31 / 20

circle 9 / 1

city 103 / 16

clam 73 / 11

clap my hands 21 / 13

clarinet 67 / 7

classroom 47 / 10

clean 11 / 18

clean up 38 / 1

clear the table 39 / 12

climb a jungle gym 55 / 14

climb a tree 55 / 18

clock 35 / 9

close your book 48 / 8

closet 35 / 17

clothes 40

cloudy 100 / 3

coach 88 / 9

coat 43 / 2

coconut 69 / 16

coffee 77 / 17

coffee table 33 / 3

cold (Feelings) 25 / 7

cold (Illnesses) 23 / 13

cold (Opposites) 11 / 5

cold (Weather) 101 / 10

collect garbage 91 / 11

farmer **87** / 17

fast **13** / 15

fat **19** / 15

father **27** / 2

faucet **37** / 14

February **5**

feed the dog **39** / 15

feelings **24**

ferret **93** / 11

fever **23** / 11

field **103** / 6

fifteen **3**

fifth **4**

fifty **3**

fight fires **91** / 19

finger **17** / 14

fire engine **81** / 10

fire station **83** / 10

firefighter **87** / 14

fireplace **33** / 13

first **4**

fish **73** / 10

fisherman **87** / 18

fishing **63** / 11

five **3**

five fifty-five **7** / 7

fix teeth **90** / 1

flag **47** / 9

floor **33** / 18

florist **86** / 5

flowers **29** / 8

flower shop **85** / 3

flute **67** / 6

fly airplanes **91** / 18

flying a kite **62** / 4

foal **95** / 17

foggy **100** / 6

fold the laundry **38** / 8

food **31** / 9

foot **17** / 19

football **58** / 3

forest **103** / 5

forest animals **96**

fork **31** / 17

forty **3**

four **3**

fourteen **3**

fourth **4**

fox **97** / 10

french fries **74** / 4

French horn **67** / 11

Friday **5**

frog **97** / 5

front yard **29** / 6

fruit **68**

fry the fish **79** / 12

full **11** / 2

G g

garage **29** / 10

garbage collector **89** / 20

garden **29** / 7

garlic **71** / 19

gas station **83** / 8

gerbil **93** / 8

giraffe **99** / 19

girl's room **47** / 3

glass **31** / 15

glasses **43** / 15

globe **47** / 15

glove (Sports
    Equipment) **61** / 5

gloves (More
    Accessories) **45** / 7

glue **51** / 1

go to the door **48** / 2

goat **95** / 12

going down **15** / 14

going up **15** / 13

goldfish **93** / 12

golf **59** / 12

golf ball **61** / 7

golf club **61** / 6

goodie bag **57** / 12

goose **95** / 8

gorilla **99** / 12

gosling **95** / 9

grandfather **27** / 6

grandmother **27** / 5

grandparents **27** / 11

grapefruit **69** / 12

grapes **69** / 4

gray hair **19** / 5

green **9** / 12

green eyes **19** / 11

grill the chicken **78** / 9

grow vegetables **90** / 9

guinea pig **93** / 9

guitar **67** / 2

gym **47** / 1

gymnastics **59** / 18

H h

hair **17** / 2

hair salon **85** / 4

hall **47** / 2

ham **73** / 6

hamburger **74** / 3

hamster **93** / 10

hand **17** / 13

handkerchief **45** / 20

happy **25** / 2

harbor **103** / 13

hard **11** / 16

harp **67** / 13

hat **43** / 14

having a campfire **62** / 7

head **17** / 1

make two lines **49** / 19

mango **69** / 20

March **5**

marker **51** / 16

Mars **106**

May **5**

me **27** / 12

meat **72**

mechanic **89** / 19

melon **69** / 10

Mercury **106**

messy **13** / 2

microwave **31** / 4

midnight **7** / 12

milk **77** / 10

mirror **35** / 3

mittens **45** / 8

mix the dressing **78** / 4

mole **97** / 6

Monday **5**

monkey **99** / 11

months **5**

Moon **106**

moose **97** / 16

mop the floor **38** / 3

more **12**

morning **7** / 8

mother **27** / 1

motorcycle **81** / 4

mountains **103** / 1

mouse **97** / 7

mouth **17** / 7

movie star **88** / 8

movie theater **85** / 6

museum **83** / 3

mushroom **71** / 16

music room **47** / 6

musical instruments **66**

N n

narrow **13** / 12

neat **13** / 1

neck **17** / 9

necklace **45** / 11

necktie **45** / 3

Neptune **107**

new **11** / 7

news reporter **88** / 4

next to **15** / 10

night **7** / 14

night table **35** / 7

nightgown **41** / 19

nine **3**

nineteen **3**

ninety **3**

ninth **4**

noisemaker **57** / 13

noodles **75** / 11

noon **7** / 11

North America **104**

nose **17** / 6

notebook **51** / 8

November **5**

numbers **3**

nurse **87** / 10

O o

occupational **90**

occupations **86**

oceans **104**

October **5**

of **16**

office (School Rooms) **47** / 8

office (Stores and
   Buildings) **83** / 7

old (Descriptions) **19** / 18

old (Opposites) **11** / 8

on **15** / 12

one **3**

one fifteen **7** / 2

one forty-five **7** / 4

one hundred **3**

one million **3**

one o'clock **7** / 1

one thirty **7** / 3

one thousand **3**

onion **71** / 20

open your book **48** / 7

opposites **10**

orange (Fruit) **69** / 11

orange (Shapes and
   Colors) **9** / 10

orange juice **77** / 13

ordinals **4**

out of **15** / 2

outdoor **62**

oval **9** / 5

oven **31** / 3

overalls **43** / 5

owl **97** / 2

oyster **73** / 9

P p

Pacific Ocean **105**

pack a lunch **79** / 19

paddle **61** / 17

paint **51** / 5

paint pictures **90** / 7

paintbrush **51** / 6

pajamas **41** / 8

pan **31** / 12

pancakes **75** / 14

panda **99** / 8

pants **41** / 3

papaya **69** / 19

paper **51** / 2

S s

sad **25** / 4
sailboat **81** / 15
sailing **63** / 14
salad **74** / 6
salesclerk **86** / 3
sandals **43** / 9
sandwich **74** / 9
Saturday **5**
Saturn **107**
saxophone **67** / 8
scale **37** / 17
scared **25** / 14
scarf **45** / 2
school **83** / 2
school rooms **46**
school supplies **50**
scientist **89** / 12
scissors **51** / 3
scooter **81** / 5
scratch my back **21** / 11
scuba diving **63** / 16
sea **103** / 12
seal **99** / 3
seasons **5**
second **4**
secretary **86** / 8
sell flowers **90** / 8
September **5**
set the table **39** / 11
seven **3**
seventeen **3**
seventh **4**
seventy **3**
sew **65** / 18
shampoo **37** / 3
shape **8**
sheep **95** / 6

shelf **35** / 15
ship **81** / 16
shirt **41** / 2
shoes **41** / 10
shopkeeper **86** / 4
short (Descriptions) **19** / 20
short (Opposites) **11** / 9
shorts **43** / 10
shoulder **17** / 10
shower **37** / 13
shrimp **73** / 12
sick **25** / 12
sidewalk **29** / 13
sing songs **90** / 6
singer **88** / 7
sink **31** / 1
sister **27** / 3
sit down **49** / 16
sit on the seesaw **54** / 8
six **3**
sixteen **3**
sixth **4**
sixty **3**
skateboard **53** / 16
ski poles **61** / 15
skiing **63** / 20
skip **55** / 19
skirt **41** / 14
skis **61** / 14
skunk **97** / 12
sleep **21** / 10
sleeping bag **61** / 12
sleepy **25** / 3
slice the cucumber **78** / 3
slide down the slide **55** / 15
slippers **41** / 20
slow **13** / 16
smile **21** / 19
snacks **76**

snake **97** / 4
snap my fingers **21** / 14
sneakers **43** / 6
sneeze **20** / 5
snowy **100** / 5
soap **37** / 4
soccer **58** / 4
soccer ball **61** / 10
socks **41** / 9
soda pop **77** / 14
sofa **33** / 2
soft **11** / 15
softball **58** / 2
Solar System **106**
sore throat **23** / 16
sour **13** / 4
South America **104**
spaghetti **74** / 2
spider **97** / 3
spinach **71** / 4
spoon **31** / 19
sports **58**
sports equipment **60**
spring **5**
square (Opposites) **11** / 4
square (Shapes and
    Colors) **9** / 2
squid **73** / 8
squirrel **97** / 13
stairs **29** / 14
stamp my feet **21** / 16
stand up **49** / 15
star (Shapes and
    Colors) **9** / 8
star (The Solar System) **106**
steak **73** / 4
steam the vegetables **78** / 7
steps **29** / 3
stereo **33** / 7

stickers 57 / 14

stir the soup 78 / 8

stomachache 23 / 9

stores 82

stormy 100 / 7

stove 31 / 2

straight hair 19 / 7

strawberries 69 / 1

streamer 57 / 9

stretch my arms 21 / 12

student 89 / 13

study 65 / 10

subway 81 / 8

suit 41 / 4

summer 5

Sun 106

sunburn 23 / 3

Sunday 5

sunglasses 45 / 9

sunny 100 / 1

supermarket 85 / 5

surfing 63 / 15

surprised 25 / 16

sushi 75 / 10

sweater 41 / 16

sweatpants 41 / 12

sweatshirt 41 / 11

sweep the floor 38 / 2

sweet 13 / 3

swimming 58 / 8

swimsuit 43 / 11

swing on the swing 54 / 9

T t

table 31 / 8

tablecloth 57 / 10

taco 74 / 7

take a bath 20 / 4

take a nap 65 / 20

take out the trash 39 / 10

take out your book 49 / 13

take pictures 90 / 4

talk on the telephone 64 / 7

tall 19 / 19

taxi 81 / 6

taxi driver 87 / 16

tea 77 / 18

teach math 90 / 3

teacher 89 / 14

teakettle 31 / 10

teddy bear 53 / 11

telephone 33 / 11

telescope 106

ten 3

ten thousand 3

tennis 59 / 10

tennis ball 61 / 2

tennis racket 61 / 1

tent 61 / 11

tenth 4

the 16

thick 13 / 5

thin (Descriptions) 19 / 16

thin (More Opposites) 13 / 6

third 4

thirsty 25 / 9

thirteen 3

thirty 3

three 3

throw a ball 55 / 10

throw a Frisbee disc 55 / 17

thunder 101 / 14

Thursday 5

tiger 99 / 13

tights 41 / 17

time 6

tissue 37 / 8

to the left of 15 / 3

to the right of 15 / 4

toast the bread 79 / 17

toaster 31 / 5

toe 17 / 20

tofu 75 / 13

toilet 37 / 15

toilet paper 37 / 16

tomato 71 / 11

toothache 23 / 8

toothbrush 37 / 1

toothpaste 37 / 2

touch the desk 48 / 4

towel 37 / 6

toys 52

toy box 35 / 1

toy store 85 / 10

track and field 59 / 14

train (Toys) 53 / 3

train (Transportation) 81 / 9

train station 83 / 11

transportation 80

tree 29 / 9

triangle 9 / 3

trombone 67 / 10

truck (Toys) 53 / 6

truck (Transportation) 81 / 3

trumpet 67 / 9

T-shirt 41 / 1

tuba 67 / 12

Tuesday 5

turkey 73 / 2

turn off the light 39 / 18

turn on the light 39 / 17

turtle 93 / 14

TV 33 / 4

twelve 3

twelve ten 7 / 6

twenty 3

twenty-one 3

two 3

two o'clock 7 / 5

U u

ugly **19** / 14
umbrella **45** / 6
uncle **27** / 8
under **15** / 11
underpants **41** / 7
undershirt **41** / 6
uniform **43** / 12
Uranus **107**
use the computer **64** / 5

V v

vacuum the carpet **38** / 4
van **81** / 2
VCR **33** / 5
vegetables **70**
Venus **106**
verbs **20**
vest **41** / 5
veterinarian **87** / 19
video **84**
video store **85** / 2
videotape **33** / 6
village **103** / 14
violin **67** / 3
volcano **103** / 2
volleyball (Sports) **58** / 6
volleyball (Sports
    Equipment) **61** / 9

W w

walk **55** / 20
walk the dog **39** / 16
wall **33** / 19
wallet **45** / 16
warm **101** / 11

wash my face **20** / 3
wash the dishes **39** / 13
wash the spinach **78** / 1
washcloth **37** / 5
wastebasket **37** / 18
watch **45** / 14
watch TV **64** / 3
water **77** / 15
waterfall **103** / 3
watermelon **69** / 9
waterskiing **63** / 17
weather **100**
weather forecaster **88** / 3
Wednesday **5**
week **5**
wet **11** / 19
whale **99** / 1
white **9** / 17
wide **13** / 11
wiggle my toes **21** / 17
window **29** / 16
windsurfing **63** / 18
windy **100** / 4
wink **21** / 18
winter **5**
worried **25** / 13
wrapping paper **57** / 6
wrestling **59** / 16
write a letter **65** / 11
write your name **48** / 9

X x

xylophone **67** / 14

Y y

yawn **20** / 9
yellow **9** / 11

yo-yo **53** / 2
yogurt **75** / 20
young **19** / 17

Z z

zebra **99** / 18
zero **3**
zipper **43** / 16
zoo animals **98**